baby's first...

Senior designer Catherine Griffin
Commissioning editor Annabel Morgan
Production Gemma Moules
Art director Anne-Marie Bulat
Editorial director Julia Charles
Publishing director Alison Starling

First published in the United States
in 2006 by Ryland Peters & Small, Inc
519 Broadway, Fifth Floor, New York NY10012
www.rylandpeters.com
10 9 8 7 6 5 4 3 2

ISBN-10: 1-84597-108-6
ISBN-13: 978-1-84597-108-3

Printed in China

RYLAND
PETERS
& SMALL

LONDON NEW YORK

baby's first...

a book to record special moments in baby's first year

place

baby's own

photograph

here

This book is for

....

from

....

date

....

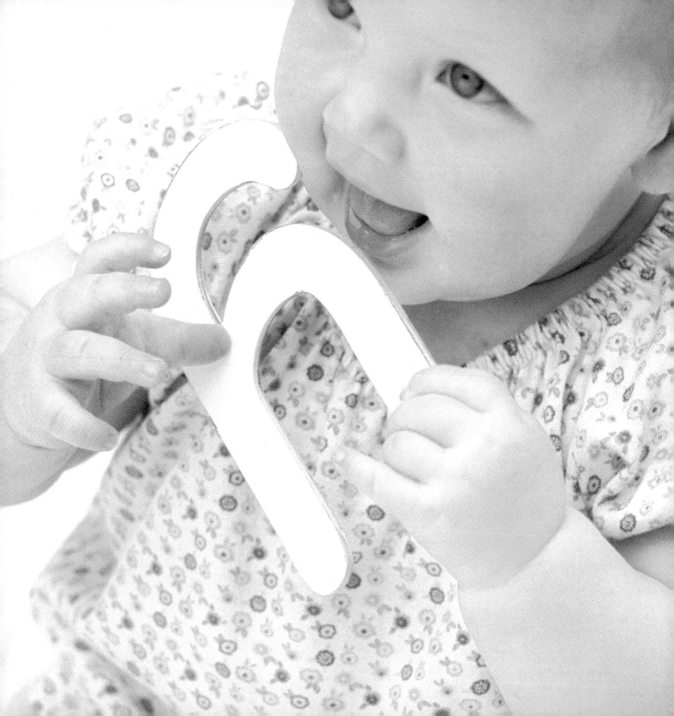

using this book

The first year of your child's life is a magical experience, and new parents vow to remember every minute of it. However, time flashes past, and all too soon your newborn is a vigorous toddler. *Baby's First...* is designed to help you record all the important events in baby's first year. Insightful questions encourage you to document baby's physical, mental, and social development right up to baby's first birthday. Try to fill in the journal as close to "real time" as possible, so that your responses are spontaneous, accurate, and vivid. When completed, *Baby's First...* will be a treasured keepsake to return to over the years, and your child will love reading all about his or her first year!

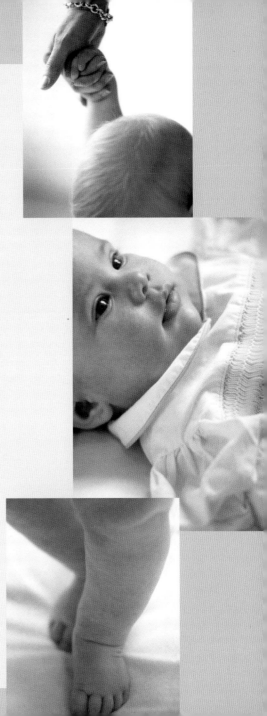

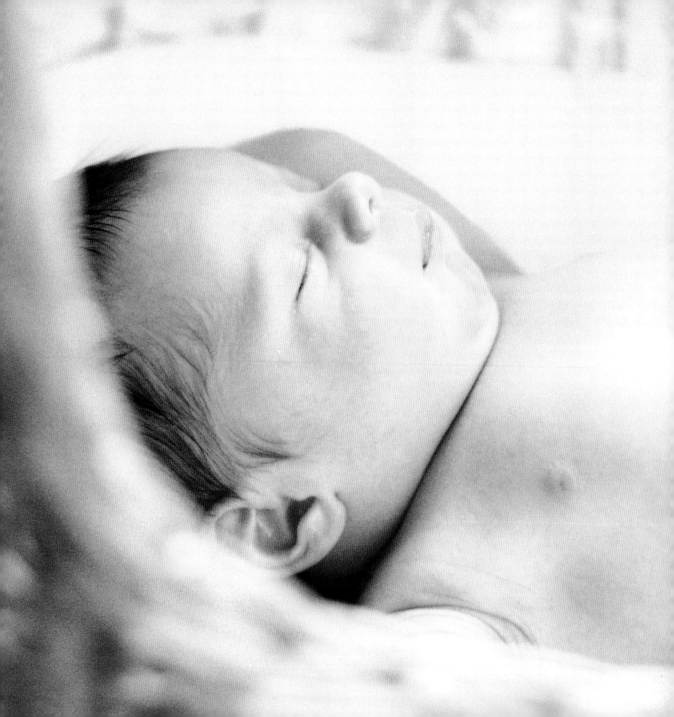

the new arrival

place ultrasound

printout or

baby's hospital

wristband here

you've arrived!

date of birth

....

time of birth

....

place of birth

....

weight

....

length

....

when we first saw you, we...
....

....

first feed   date:
....
....
....
....
....
....

first bath   date:
....
....
....
....
....
....

first visitors   date:

....

....

....

....

....

....

first gifts
....

everyone's
gathered
here to
meet you

....

....

....

....

....

....

time to settle in

first trip in a car .... date: ....

....

....

....

....

first night at home .... date: ....

....

....

....

....

first outing in your stroller
....
date:
....

....

....

....

....

....

....

....

....

....

....

....

baby's first handprint

baby's first footprint

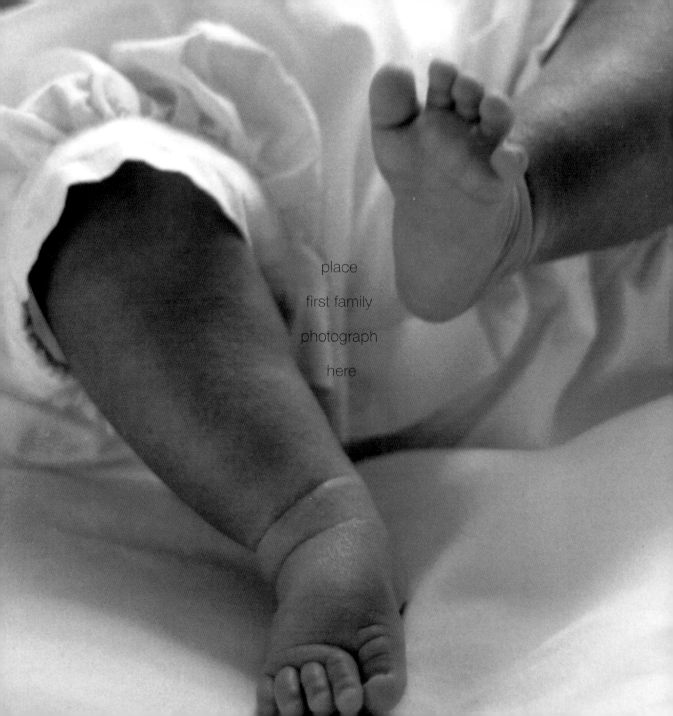

place

first family

photograph

here

growing and changing

first focused eyes
....

date:
....

....

....

....

....

....

....

first followed object with eyes
....

date:
....

....

....

....

....

....

....

becoming aware
of your world...

first held up head
....

date:
....

....

....

....

....

....

first smiled
....

date:
....

....

....

....

....

....

first tried to grasp a toy

date:

first grasped and held a toy

date:

first found your thumb   date:

....

....

....

....

....

....

first found your feet   date:

....

....

....

....

....

....

finding your feet

first cooed   date:
....
....
....
....
....
....

first laughed   date:
....
....
....
....
....
....

first babbled   date:

....

....

....

....

....

....

....

....

....

....

....

do I make
myself
clear?

a change to the menu

first taste of solids   date:

....

....

....

....

first drink from a sippy cup   date:

....

....

....

....

first finger foods   date:

....

....

....

....

first clapped

....

date:

....

....

....

....

....

show me how it's done....

....

....

....

....

....

....

....

first waved goodbye
....
date:
....

....

....

....

....

....

....

first pointed
....
date:
....

....

....

....

....

....

....

first rolled over   date:

....

....

....

....

....

....

first sat up   date:

....

....

....

....

....

....

first crawled on belly   date:

....

....

....

....

....

first crawled on knees   date:

....

....

....

....

....

I'm on the move!

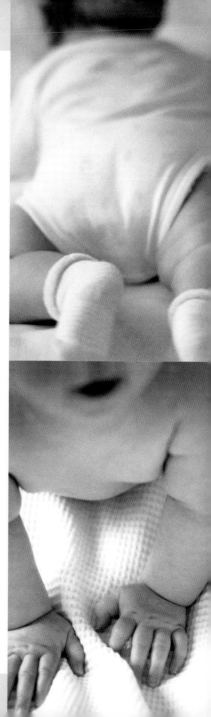

first pulled yourself up to stand   date:
....

....

....

....

....

first stood unaided   date:
....

....

....

....

first walked unaided   date:
....

....

....

....

there's no stopping me now!

magical milestones

first night in your own room   date:
....

....

....

....

....

....

first meal in a highchair   date:

....

....

....

....

....

....

becoming independent

first used a spoon   date:

....

....

....

....

....

first medical check   date:
....

....

who was the pediatrician?
....

....

how much did I weigh?
....

....

what tests did I have?
....

....

what shots did I have?
....

....

....

....

I'm looking different every day!

first haircut   date:

....

....

....

....

....

....

....

first tooth   date:

....

....

....

....

....

....

....

first little friends

....

....

....

....

....

....

....

....

....

....

....

....

....

first pair of shoes   date:

....

....

....

....

on my own two feet...

first said mama
....

date:
....

....

....

....

....

....

first said dada
....

date:
....

....

....

....

....

....

I love mommy and daddy!

first kissed mommy

....

date:

....

....

....

....

....

....

....

first kissed daddy

....

date:

....

....

....

....

....

....

....

first family vacation   date:
....

we went to...
....

....

our journey was...
....

....

....

we stayed at...
....

....

....

we saw...
....

....

....

....

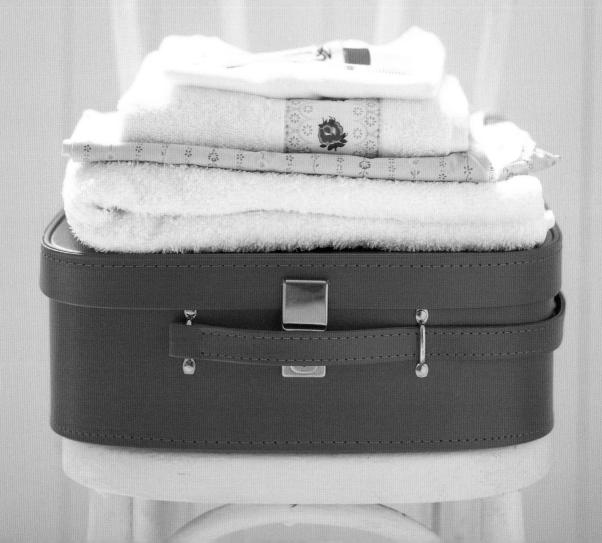

let's take a trip together...

first birthday   date:

....

....

....

....

....

....

....

....

what gifts did I receive?

....

....

....

....

what's all the fuss about?

first christmas or hanukkah

....

....

....

....

....

....

what gifts did I receive?

....

....

....

....

picture credits

All photography by Debi Treloar, except 33 by Lena Ikse-Bergman, and page 12

background © Stockbyte.